Conversations with Trees

poems by

Susan Dambroff

Finishing Line Press
Georgetown, Kentucky

Conversations with Trees

Copyright © 2018 by Susan Dambroff
ISBN 978-1-63534-427-1 First Edition
All rights reserved under International and Pan-American Copyright Conventions. No part of this book may be reproduced in any manner whatsoever without written permission from the publisher, except in the case of brief quotations embodied in critical articles and reviews.

ACKNOWLEDGMENTS

Thank you to the following publications where these poems have previously appeared, sometimes in slightly different forms.

Oxygen: "Lost and Found"
Poets 11: "To Taste the Beauty," "New Year," "To Put Back Belief"
Poetry San Francisco: "For My Father I fill the Hospital Room with Trees"

Much gratitude to all those who have intimately shared in my creative journey. Amongst them are Kimi Sugioka, Amy Cooper, Kathleeen Byrne, Chris Kammler, and Jeff Demark. And my deepest thanks to the Lost Coast Writer's Retreat and the members of my San Francisco Writing Group for their ongoing support and inspiration. I am indebted to Maureen Roggow of Writer's Wings, and David Tuller for their help with the daunting process of submissions and editing, and to Finishing Line Press for their gift of recognition. And to my loving partner Janice Strassheim and our daughter Natalie Strassheim, who have shaped so many of the memories that have become these poems.

Publisher: Leah Maines
Editor: Christen Kincaid
Cover Art: Susan Dambroff
Author Photo: Natalie Strassheim
Cover Design: Elizabeth Maines McCleavy

Printed in the USA on acid-free paper.
Order online: www.finishinglinepress.com
           also available on amazon.com

                    Author inquiries and mail orders:
                         Finishing Line Press
                            P. O. Box 1626
                     Georgetown, Kentucky 40324
                               U. S. A.

Table of Contents

A New Year 1

Taste the Beauty 2

Lost and Found 4

Incomprehensible Wounds 5

Lately 6

Letter to a Birthmother 8

Rivers Poem 10

Ladder 11

Eulogy 13

An Unexpected Distance 15

Writers in a Pavilion of Trees 16

Introvert 17

The Same Poem 19

All I Don't Know but Wonder 20

Everything That Bloomed 22

Beloved 24

Vast 25

For My Father 26

*For Amy and Kim
and for all the trees
that have taken root
in every poem*

A New Year

After the argument about putting the top back on the toothpaste
we will get dressed and out the door
alive enough and ready for cars and forecasts of rain
ready to orchestrate food radio and gasoline
to drink our 8 glasses of water
to crave a bite of chocolate
to navigate the day through the hieroglyphs of a date book
alive enough for cell phone interruptions
for red light aggravations
alive enough for patience
impatience
for noticing in the doctor's waiting room the old man with glasses
with the impish smile of my father
alive enough to miss him so terribly gone
and seeing the woman riding a bicycle
beneath a familiar canopy of trees
with the piercing eyes of my mother
her face pouched with uncertainty
alive enough to remember that mix of worry and love
to take a deep breath into the rise of eucalyptus
that takes me back
to that apartment where love was a young body
standing by an open window with a bare and proud chest
alive enough for time's recognition
for the pause between placing the apples in the shopping cart
and noticing the outrageous price of blueberries
the drifting image of sunrise on a New Hampshire mountain
in the summer
my small hands picking blueberries on the trail
alive enough to push the shopping cart to the next aisle
to pick up a new tube of toothpaste
to remember the story about the dying woman who wished
she could taste again
the ripeness of a tomato
alive enough to let the argument go

Taste th Beauty

this city in a cold rain
the mother who yells at her son
saying she should have had a puppy instead
life is too short to save
the sunrise before work
the neighbor cat perched on the front stoop
like a postcard

my mother says when I was a child
all she had to do was put me on the floor
with a doll
and I'd be content
now I'm a restless old cat
pacing
the same distance between home and work
liquor store
auto parts store
bookshelves made to order
where am I going
from dreams
to sore hip
my mother limping into old age
the same view out my window
rooftop
chimney
laundromat
the man ranting down the street
that he'd like to do to the opposite sex
what Hitler did to the Jews
telephone wire
parked car
this familiar fight
in the back of my throat
my mother tells me she had four cardiograms
to find out her heart had moved
street signs
street lights

life is too short to save
the kiss of a baby
sweet like a cinnamon roll
I need more than a supermarket line
the green borders of a city block
where dogs romp from one tree to the other
while owners open their collar buttons
to deep sigh their work day away

to just imagine that every day is my last
all the carved faces
a sudden beauty
the boy who holds his backpack like a prize

Lost and Found

under some theater I lost the green stone around my neck
the hand of god lost the resin in my voice

     in a pumpkin patch without parents or language she lost
the weight of a hand holding her lost the still backyard
her mother's shoes the daughter I was

I found a glass door a porched thought a circle of lapis inside
a backpack found a yellow house with a palm tree view
lost track of my wounds found her slipping silently
through the glass

     found a mountain a white haired woman on a wet rock
behind a city gathering watercress found a totem of a fish bird
woman a sprig of sage

     on my doorstep found a package found a woman in the
hospital who was missing a package found my brother's name
across my back my mother's ancient stitches lost the pin to my
father's watch lost the weight of a hand holding me found
the little girl eating her hair to get full

     lost the roots of the cypress under the leaves of sleep
the black cat night lost the way out the staircase beneath
my bed found jewels in the eyes of animals found flowers
on the pillows of death found her lost bones frolicking
across my ceiling

Incomprehensible Wounds

Out this window
winter apples
still hold
This is where I begin—
Yesterday I read stories
about mothers
drowning their newborn girls
over and over
the boy
the land
the food
the family name
to continue
in each goodbye
harbored
in the bodies of women
who try to remember
try to forget
the baby girls
left at train stations
outside of hospitals
All that sorrow
in each goodbye
held back
My Chinese daughter
left on the courthouse steps
the mother she comes from
so dimpled and lovely
The mother I am
because of the mother she couldn't be
Incomprehensible Wounds

Lately

my old cat sleeps
in my poems
sleeps beneath her sky blue blanket
in all of my poems
lately
I don't remember my dreams
only that I am forever losing something
worth having
the tree cut
from my window
a sneaker wave
that suddenly
takes me away
lately
I have been craving chocolate
some rush of imagination
I am thigh high
in the unknown
some math without answer
lately I dream autistic children
have long sentences of explanation
I try to read a book in your eyes
lately there is something I want
without asking
like the cat
who gets held
and stroked
and talked to
without asking
lately
I look for myself
in your arms
remember the smell

of what hurt
like parents
who will never come back
from that long drive
across town
lately
I am oceans of fear
the rain that held its breath
for years
and finally fell

Letter to a Birthmother

I am seven years old.
I miss you.
I am going to China when I am 10.
I want to see you.

With a long white candle
she burns the letters in a clay bowl
staring at the flame

Then she begins to write some more
I hope you are not sad.
Thank you for giving me my mom.

We watch the smoke rise
talk about how a heart
can speak into the air

Then she pulls weeds
wrangles with the blackberry bushes
digs and digs until the roots come out

We take the ashes from the bowl
and spread them under a tree
we tell her we don't know who her birthmother is
we tell her that when we go to China
we don't think we will find her

She says
What if she was walking down the street
How would we know who she was?
What if she was wearing a bow?
Then could we find her?

When she is done in the garden
she wants to wash her feet
like they do in the movie
about families from China
I bring her a bowl with soapy water
and we begin to scrub

At dinner we eat take-out Chinese food
put everything in the center of the table
and reach our chopsticks in

Rivers Poem

My brother proudly took us out
on his boat on the Hudson River
It was all about
the speed at which he could travel
I held my small daughter close
as we churned through the water
in some kind of hurry I didn't share
So much holding on in that journey
I could hardly notice
the wide open around me
By then I had already moved
to California
where hills and water
stretched into vast possibilities
At the Russian River
I found
the perfect balance
between trees and water
The strong stance of the redwoods
the deep pull of the current
I walked slept floated back
to young timeless summers
renewed and reminded
of simple desires
banks of August blackberries
quiet roads where my daughter
learned to ride her bicycle
The house we rented
its dock
with an old green canoe
and all of us
taking our sweet time
paddling down the river

Ladder

A space that opens before me
a room where a window faces out
becomes a journey over the hill
I once lay in a bathtub
under layers of trees
contemplating morning glories
stood under an outdoor shower
watching black and white cows
grazing an open field

When even the past can be rearranged
when what gets remembered
is not the insatiable longing
for a love that's gone
for the long strands of blonde hair
no longer left in my bed
but instead the spark
of that first date
the nectarine she placed in my hand
like a promise

Not the yearning
for all the animals who died young
but the warm smoky fur of the cat
that for 20 years
nestled on my heart

Not the thought
that I will never have
another first love
but how the young man I thought I would marry
still often sleeps beside me
in my dreams

To fall into the future
the best unknown
how my garden will replace me
how the wild roses I planted last year
have already blossomed
and the forget-me-nots
will someday become
the carpet of blue
I imagined

To know that change will come
with certainty
my lover of 25 years
puts wisps of purple
across her graying hair
my daughter who will never have my eyes
once fit her small feet
inside my hands

Eulogy
> *for Kim*

I want to name everything
you loved
persimmons and quince blossoms,
Meyer lemons and blackberries,
cats and redwood trees,
poems by Mary Oliver,
all the words to Motown,
the way the sun
would make its way back
after a long rain

The spirit of places and things
that mattered
Russian River,
Goat Rock Beach,
gallery in Bodega Bay,
museums in San Francisco,
vineyards with perfectly spaced lines,
the persimmon tree out your kitchen window,
an orange tile etched with the Chinese character for "courage",
Japanese prints of bridges and rain,
sticky notes on your mirror,
I am healthy, I am strong
I will live to see Obama elected

And all the people
you loved
adamantly and
generously
friends from the gym,
around the Bridge table,
on Facebook,
the ones you were young with,
wanted to grow old with,
who cooked the best Italian,
who baked the most beautiful cakes,
the brother who made everything better,
babies born soon enough
for you to hold

I see you now
rising up in the hot air balloon
you always wanted
your yippeeee
hovering over the glaciers of Alaska
eyes wide with delight
calling out the words
you always used
to say goodbye
Know that I love you

An Unexpected Distance

Corinne with her white hair
and blue eyes
stretched out her arms
and jumped off the overpass
as if flying
how she chose to land on the tracks
not the road
didn't want to hurt anyone else
who might drive into her

We land an unexpected distance
from where we start out
a breath caught while walking up a city hill
the heart breaks between beats
but you think you can retrieve yourself

Lucy lay down on a tarp
in a bed of leaves
so she could easily be lifted
and taken away
she left her lover the letters
pasted on the scrabble board
I will always love you
then wrote a letter to the coroner
telling exactly where
she could be found

I look across the fence
to the tree
that holds Corinne's apples
green and waiting for her
to pick
remembering the bags she would leave
by our door
plump with potatoes and garlic
with a note that said
blessings

Writers in a Pavilion of Trees

between leaves
a soliloquy into silence
slides the pen
into vastness

a forgotten lift of the heart
rises up with the pines
landscapes call
the pen to travel

she marvels
a thought between her eyes

he rubs his chin
gives homage to the page
and to the field

senses speak to curiosity

the insistent call of a bird
and the curls of sound
rearranged in answer

Introvert

When I was a child
I didn't talk to grown ups
never thought I'd be one
stared at the trees
that became my language

Sometimes it's too hard
to navigate periphery
but when there's intimacy of story
I commit to it
with an easiness of words
rapidly firing in exchange

I've learned a lot about the expected
niceties of social discourse
but still have difficulty
saying goodbye to people at parties
just have to slip out the back door
to find myself again

I return to the honesty
of my own landscape
my old studio apartment
emptied of the past
dreamt about over and over
holding to potted plants
on the fire escape
my cats long gone
lazing in the sun
staring at the overgrown garden
that kept them wild

And in the corner of the room
my old electric typewriter
tracking my joys and wounds

What matters most about solitude
the soul finding its instruction
softly

This is not loneliness
this is the uncompromised hum
that connects me back

The Same Poem

I write the same poem over and over
what I've lost so many times before

Childhood with an open mitt
the ball on a fly
my father's freckled hands
teaching me overhand and underhand

I try to get things back
my young body rolling down a grassy hill
dizzy joy as the sky turns over

This poem again and again
growing up beneath an electrical tower
that might fall on me in the night
the ritual of prayers
to some God
I needed to name

Finding the corner no one else wanted
writing on small scraps of paper
in the pantry
trying to find space
between my mother's muddled life
and mine

What I revisit with new words
a change in the space of a line
taking me further than I remembered

I write back my childhood
in the view of a thousand autumn trees
all the different shades of dying
before the road got carved between them
and the silence
that was speckled with birds
became forever changed

All I Don't Know but Wonder

That wooly hill
that tender wind gesturing
the trees
the field that divides with shadow
speckled yellow dandelions
that bring me back
to wide delights
young summers
the immensity of time

The line the blanket made
across the grass
where I wrote letters
propped on elbows
in a field
folding envelopes into story
the length of August

The bark of birch trees
unraveling into precious scrolls
and dandelions
gone to seed
blown into prayers

And back to here
the red cottage
my pile of books
pen and paper
all I don't know
but wonder

Wings and stems
blossoms and chatter
pecking pecking
the leaf that falls
without question or answer

And the line the blanket made
across the grass
my thoughts loosening
in the steamy heat
words enveloped
into silence

To have this be
my instruction
to sit in a field of dandelions in June
and not know more or better
to be dropped into plenty
without answer or question
the bee buzzing as it does

Everything That Bloomed

my mother
with thigh up on couch
smell of linoleum
glint in her eye
says
growing old is for the birds

I remember everything that bloomed
one yellow rose beneath my window
azaleas bordering the front door

there was always sugar in her cup
instant coffee with lots of milk
at the kitchen table
pale pink paper napkins
and the ridges of a flower
I could trace
with a pen

everything held in my small hand
birch bark curled around a finger
buttercups under my chin
then my daughter
in the garden
with grandma's chalky ashes
falling from her palm

what remains
in the knots of the pine walls
of the kitchen
everything laid out on our plates
farmer's cheese and crackers
deep red cherries
cashews
the tales of her young dark beauty
wrapped in a box of costumes
from Radio City Music Hall
and between the spines of
Dorothy Parker and Emily Dickinson
and inside the mysteries of Agatha Christie
propped on the rumpled pillows of her bed
she stretches out
her shiny worn feet

and I see her
still
driving me home
up the long slope of driveway
where the dogwood petals
scatter on the roof
like snow

Beloved

To put it simply
We are too measured
in our love
What I want
my interior life
shared
To ask it simply
Do you want that too?
What means this word beloved?
The way we gaze
at our elm's magnificence
To put it simply
There will be days
we both won't belong
to this world
anymore
Can we untangle our logic
and meet
at the heart?

Vast

This house with its red door and everything it opens into, cut flowers
on the kitchen table and the field that grew them, letters that find words
that find poems that cheer the heart, window that faces a hill,
a rope swing on a tree, a child flying out with abandon, a staircase
walk to a full moon, all Gods we follow, conjure, question, prayers
for safe passage, to beckon the rain, insisting on beauty, wild roses,
hills fresh with snow, everything possible, stars we don't yet know,
vast and incomprehensible, insisting on love's bravery, we go on

For My Father:
> *I Fill the Hospital Room with Trees*

For you
from whom I learned
to love the trees
      I light the candles
blue and green
are for healing
and red
is for the heart

I take this walk
for you
a green walk
into
your heart
I do not doubt
the trees
they are not bones
but muscles
holding up the sky

I am sitting down
with you
against this tree
      who was it
      who said
if you lean against a tree
and breathe it
into your back
it brings your two lives
together

Susan Dambroff is a poet, performer and teacher. She shares her San Francisco life with her partner Janice, their daughter Natalie, and Harold, their beloved mutt. She has just completed a long and rich career in Special Education in the San Francisco public school system, where she engaged in mutual acts of discovery with children and families.

Her creative and spiritual life is continually informed by the presence of nature. She is forever grateful to the 100-year-old elm that blesses her urban backyard and inspires daily acts of witness. This process of intentional noticing has inhabited her writing as well as her photography. As she compiled *Conversations with Trees* from poems that weave back and forth from childhood to the present, she was reminded of how trees have always fed her spirit and have taken root in her poetic imagination.

Her first book of poems, entitled *MEMORY IN BONE*, was published in a letterpress edition by Black Oyster Press. Her work has been included in several anthologies of Holocaust writings, including *Blood to Remember* (Time Being Books), *Ghosts of the Holocaust* (Wayne State University Press), and Images from the Holocaust (NTC Publishing Group). Most recently, her poems have appeared in *Stoneboat, Red Bird Chapbooks,* and *Earth's Daughters*.

She performs throughout the San Francisco Bay Area in *Spoken Duets*, a poetic and improvisational collaboration with performance artist Chris Kammler.